THE CHANGING COLOURS OF MY HEART

DEBJANI CHATTOPADHYAY

Copyright © Debjani Chattopadhyay
All Rights Reserved.

ISBN 979-888521304-2

This book has been published with all efforts taken to make the material error-free after the consent of the author. However, the author and the publisher do not assume and hereby disclaim any liability to any party for any loss, damage, or disruption caused by errors or omissions, whether such errors or omissions result from negligence, accident, or any other cause.

While every effort has been made to avoid any mistake or omission, this publication is being sold on the condition and understanding that neither the author nor the publishers or printers would be liable in any manner to any person by reason of any mistake or omission in this publication or for any action taken or omitted to be taken or advice rendered or accepted on the basis of this work. For any defect in printing or binding the publishers will be liable only to replace the defective copy by another copy of this work then available.

To my late brother Roni

Who taught me the courage of the stars,

With Love

Contents

Contents

Contents

Preface

An Ode to Poetry

A poet always seems insane
Whom all tries to disdain
What is clarity to them
To others
It can be vaguely lame
They make their tragedy into remedy
Not many can understand this rhapsody
Their glooming hay make sense
They throw their heart over fence
Look through their lens
You will find their valuable pens

Acknowledgements

A gentle push and a lot of love can create wonders. That's exactly what some people did to me. Therefore, I'd like to convey my gratitude to these precious few who helped me tremendously to convert this dream into reality.

To my beautiful family! My dear husband Somnath Chattopadhyay, my sweetheart daughter Samadrita Chattopadhyay and my parents Subrata Mukherjee and Sandhya Mukherjee: Thank you so much for always encouraging me in every step of the way and pushing me for the betterment. Thank you for being who you are. You guys are my rock.

A special thanks to Meenal Agarwal who stood beside me throughout this rollercoaster journey and gave me this very idea to publish this collection of poems into a book. You are a gem of a person.

Anusua Ghosh Biswas and Astha Dube who put up with my strange moods and love me unconditionally. Thank you for always being there for me.

Last but not the least, a huge thanks to my readers who gave me the courage to make this book possible. For giving me the energy that I always needed. I wouldn't trade you for anything in this world.

Dusk

Listen carefully
To the sound
Of the stillness
Like a heartbeat
Of my madness
You will find a calmness
Please don't cheat
Close your eyes
And feel the heat
Of my remembrance
Of what I had
And what I lost
You will surely
Find a cause

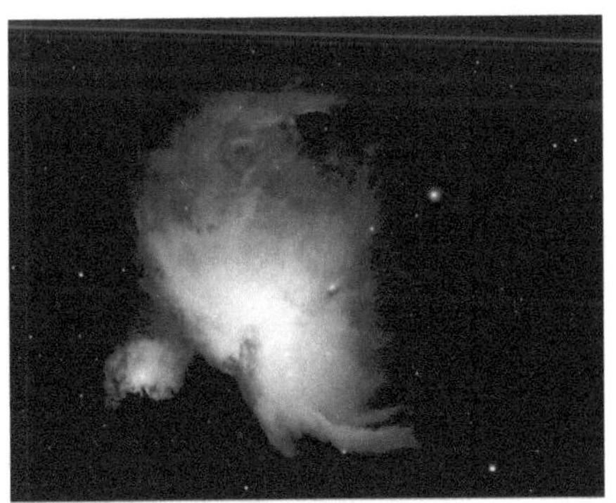

1. Home, an Odyssey

Home is not always a place
Wired with emotions
Noticed your absence
Brain haywire
Love the feeling of lost
The numbness, the lull
All signs of storms
Accumulating to burst
Comfortably caged
Not wanting to fly
For flying means
I'll touch the sky
What you call home
The Starlights guide me
When I search my way
To reach somewhere
Someone awaits for me
I consider my home

2. Endless Game

If heart aches in an unnatural whim
You fall down to your knees
Crash against the waves
So unpleasant it seems
Rustling sounds of whisper
Throughout the leaves
Parts of me getting lost
In the trembling sheets
The unsettling feeling
Of drenched heart
Shattered around
Lying in a heap of dirt
Who is there to gather it around?
No expectations whatsoever
Can't be a clown!
Again and again!
It's an endless game
Trying to be a braveheart
Far from being complacent

3. The Shadows of Abyss

Been tired as hell of late
Don't remember
The last time when I smiled fake
I was told once
If something's wrong
Should trust my star's trance
No! I don't wanna talk about myself
But it hurts
I don't even recall
When it start

Tired of falling apart
You were a powerful breeze
To be reckon with
I am still on my bruised knees
Like a tide
We used to make a mess
I am pinned with this weight
I thought you'd keep me safe
The heaviness that my heart holds
Maybe it belongs to gravity that bolts
Near-death cliches
My heart replays
Can I flip a switch
To fix a broken bridge
Before it shut down
To leave the rust behind
Nothing prepared me
For the sudden call
Vivid as a daydream
Like a freefall
Let's waste time again
In a true sense
We'd do it all again
Where happiness began
I know, I say too much
But trust me, it's not enough
Let's chase cars

And play in the garden
Where the tinge of orange
Used to peek around our heads
How many pages I turned
The way I used to
Or I am
Somethings will never change
But I don't give a damn!

4. Bleeding Soul

We were born and raised together
And together we lived more
We should have made more memories
As I am coming up with empty hands
Where are you now
When I need you the most?
Can you see from the stars
That I'm burning like a coal?
They say burn like a coal
So that you can be a diamond
But what is a diamond
Without it's shine!
Long to see our glory days again
But coming up with thin white lines
Do you recall the paths
The babbling brooks
The things we left behind
The stone bears our memories still
You captured my heart
It's not for my keeping
All belongs to the star

DEBJANI CHATTOPADHYAY

You're a shore of my soul
I'll be returning in spaces for evermore

5. Way to the Stars

Found myself drowning
One fine morning
But that's when I could finally breathe
Consumed by the fire before
Couldn't reach the shore
Kept screaming in nothingness
Though I was lifeless
The world was greener
In a world consist of you
Now it's just words
Full of hollow askews
You still exist between these lines
You'll be immortal
In my aching vines
Now I roam around in my ruined castle
Strong yet fragile
Witnessed the destructions
Through my eyes
Wearing a crown like a queen
But the crown is made of thorns
Now my blood is clean
Only the resilience left

DEBJANI CHATTOPADHYAY

Even amid the tempest
Gentle heart with hundred scars
Only graceful souls knows
How to light the way to the stars

6. Strange Astronomy

Destruction made the greenery today
Had to lose too much
This game is nasty
I had to lose my sanity
Now I speak in poetry

Try to write philosophical converse
Mental status in poetic verse
Was this worth it?
To lose you and gain this?
If I could reverse everything
I would
Just to hold you again
It is long due
This astronomy where angel sings
Is it better than the innocence
We used to bring?
Now it just stings
For now I have only doubts
Demons are fighting all day out
I am willing to reject all these
To see you again
Sometimes I lose my shit
And write all these in vain

7. Poetry in my Heart

The burden of acceptance
All of the dirt and the gifts
Of a broken human
Is it too much to ask?
Agony is unbearable sometimes
Invade us unexpected ways
A prayers is nothing
But a balloon of hope
The world is opaque
A kind of cocoon
Love is like a lava
Think before you jump
Visions are seldom
What they seems
Yet words are momentous
Unknown are the reasons
Of becoming a poet
Fasten the soften heart
Perhaps with a rivet

8. Church of Scars

You were a deceit
Like a black hole, a discreet
A deception, mere misfit
Rotating on its axis
It's a wonderland without alice
Can she survive without malice?
She has grown into silence
Mere absence without violence
A world made of resemblance
Cognizant of vengeance
You can be diligent
But yet be stringent
Now the sky cries with her
Breaks with her
Cascade her
With penetrating rain
Damn the pain!
Waiting for a fast car
Who can take her to Mars
She wants to go far
From her church of scars

9. Inner War

In order to be irreplaceable
One must be different
Our past may shape us
But it doesn't define who we become
Consultation, degradation
Immigration, stupefied
Truth is only hearsay
We're just left to decay
I got the jones right through my bones
Staying controversial
Just for the hell of it
Modernity has failed us
The war has been incited and
Guess what?
You're all invited!

10. Ricochet Love

Speechless as I am
Love ricochet, but damn!
Secret language unspoken to anyone
Kind to all, but unfair to me hun?
Laughing but the jokes not even funny!
The world seem so uncanny
Trying to fit in
But can never change the ending
Don't know why I'm so mad
And I truly regret that
Don't know what life will bring
There is some invisible strings
Tying you and me
Dream of some epiphany
Which I can't speak about
You know that I hate the crowd
Hate the feeling of this shroud
Became ash from your fire
My winless flight had the desire
To dive in the pyre
To be your martyr

11. Love is the Antidote

Sipping pink glaze
Living in a haze
Thinking out loud
What went wrong
When words came out
For you it's easy to say
Blaming is curse
For you I'm always the one
Whom you can trust
Cause lovely was the weather
When love was in the air
Now it's just a bloom
Without it's flavour
For me love is the antidote
Of all the curse
For me you are the endgame
Forever
Like an infinite universe

12. Shades of Grey

Eyes and opinions dark raven black
Fits like a glove
Too bad at love
Colours disappear
When the wheels steer
Only shades of grey remains
Borderline strangers
Still so close
Yet so far
Reflection change
Fiery glances exchange
Echoes of whisper burn holes
Charring down my heart
Lost in my mind
All the faces blurred
So used to losing
Can't hold on anymore
Rather let it wash away
Far away
After several fall
It doesn't hurt at all
At the foot of the mountains

DEBJANI CHATTOPADHYAY

It's true!
Can't love again

13. Piece of Mind

She rather stay in pieces
Than burn the bridges
Happiness is all she misses
Her scars deserves feathery kisses
She withers around gypsy flowers
Silence beneath the big enchanted cypress
Her only cover
The wind under her wings
Makes her fly

Curious butterflies hovers
She cries over empty heart
Lying on the edges
Fireflies show her light
When she loses her flight
Over the ledges
She keeps grudges at bay
It makes her wing falter
As devil preys
She thrives around rainbows
Over the dark clouds
Set aside the darkness
For it makes her doubt
And when she dances
Like a bird of paradise
She drizzles love
And hope all over
And look for the sunrise

14. Strange Dynamics

Pain lingers, but love stays
Hurting numbers are mere days
Write too many things on your way
People change and love greys
Permanent sound of laughter
Perfect irony slays
Tried to fill the bullet holes
But blood still oozes out
These types of scars
Never really gauze
Neither a stranger, nor a friend
I couldn't really penned
How an ally become fiend
The sound of your voice
Still lure me to the edge
The emotions that binds
My soul
Revert me in dread

15. Break the Barrier

Not afraid of criticism
Doesn't affect me anymore
No matter what you do
They will show the door
They might say
Write about your love life
Then they will talk rubbish
Behind your backside
If I write about heartbreak
They'll say you're trashhead
If I choose happiness finally
They'll be jealous definitely
And when I write about sorrow
They'll be like don't pretend to be hollow!
One day I wrote about my loss
They pitied me at my own cost
So I dared to speak the truth
They brand this as uncouth
So I let it be
I let it go
Let them criticise me more
Didn't let them stop me

From expressing my thoughts
I let my soul shine
Through my words

The Pink Sky

Fallen, but not broken
Forgiving, but not forgotten
I learned the art of flying
In the act of falling
It was a divine calling
In the art of breaking
I was concealing
Though it taught me
The magic of healing

16. Empathy

When light doesn't quite
Reach me anymore
Everything seem so bleak
Heart wants to find solace
And
Eyes search for peace
I still find you
Inside
That corner of my heart
Where I have buried
So many thoughts
There is a draught
Memories
That I can't seem to forget
But don't be misled
You make my inside glow
When I go brilliantly dull
Erasing my lull
No! You ain't a criminal
Just take the pain away
Somehow make it better

Heart still want to fight for it
Traverse in measure

17. Kryptonite

Like a river
Life goes on
Like watching a movie scene
We together
With all that chemistry
Became one atom by atom
With a powerful love
Most people couldn't even fathom
You're my kryptonite
Demonstrated by my whole life
Is there a thing called fulfilment
In this modern love?
I admit
Love is complicated
But it keeps me alive
It's just engraved in soul
In your bones
Layering with every inch of your skin
It's an exquisite feeling
But yet doomed
Like yin and yang
Or

Fire and ice
It's all about balance
Yes! It's a challenge
In this strange world
Where everything is in currency
Love is my vanity
The center of my gravity

18. Roses and Sprinkles

Love me

With all my flaws

As I am not perfect

See me

In all my bruised glory

For I bloom in neglect

Draw me

If you can

As you see me

With broken wings

Though I tried very hard

To fly with instinct

I'm not all roses and sprinkles
But with lots of hidden wrinkles
Give me your best
As I will give you
My all interest

19. Amore

Let me flow through thy veins
Like poetry rhythm
Make my heart sing your name
Can I be your dame?
My world revolves around love
Tears at dusk
Oh love! Don't make a fuss
Sky can be grey
Stars can go astray
You and me
Are made of clay
A beautiful portrait
When sun meets the shore
Of dancing waves
The golden glitter it arrays
That's my friend
Is called
Amore

20. Fire and Ice

There's an ocean
Full of love
In my heart
Moonlight filled the room
Of my vivid dreams
With its light
It was an idyllic love
For it made a mess too
Waves lifted like highrise
Rain followed through
I built the floodgate alone
For I've known this long ago
They will bind you in conditions
In order to keep you flow
Darkness made me realise of my value
Lent me the knowledge of true light
Comatose in the heart of sun
Stagnant views of our days
Burned from the desire of many ways
It ignited the fire in my bones
Ocean flooded my veins
Icy cold my heart

Fire and ice
A deadly combination
But a sheer magnet
Luxury is to meet an old soul
Who softly touch your scars
Not poke like others
Help to create new memories
To rewrite the stories
Hold them close if you find one
Who makes you laugh unguarded
That's how love started
Yin attracts only to yang
Bravely kiss many frogs
To find the one

21. Patterns of Madness

Now we are here
Now we don't
Fading doesn't take time
It happens in blink of an eye
Borrowed time
Biased thoughts
Glossy eyes
Poetic mind
All forms are patterns of madness
But you have to be insane
To view the rainbow
With naked eyes
To feel the rain
With bare feet
To love a little more
With the depth of your heart
Don't be afraid to be mad
As then only
You can find the rhythm
Of a silent night
Trust the vibe
To feel the light

Faith is fulfilled
If gratitude is followed
We will meet again
Until the beacon of light
Becomes hollowed

22. Elixir

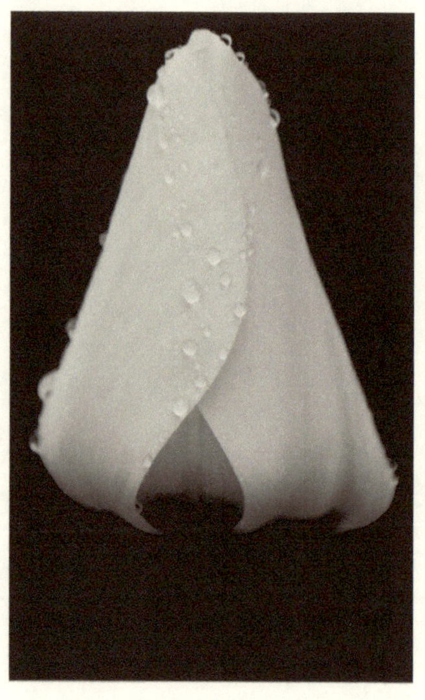

Be with someone
Who can be your
Elixir of life
With whom you can soar higher

Like a phoenix from past's ashes
Who can give an unique taste
To every places you visit
To break the monotony
Of everyday's digit
Who can make you see the sun
When your eyes are covered
In watery haze
Who can make you feel enchanted
Under the moonlight's daze
And this who
You can be too!
Rather than waiting for someone
You can make your own elixir anew!

23. Floating Conflict

There's a magic in her madness
A fire in her simple things
How powerful and complex
Her mind is
The small things makes
This world unique
Several in the galaxy
Fascinating it is
Love is the heart of all
Floating in a conflict

24. Pain vs Pleasure

Part of me died long ago
Only the ashes remains
The fire is numbed
Memories are dumped
Got better at losing things
Now I ignore blings
Cause my visions are moist
Do I have a choice?
Used to build castles
Among stars
Used to see twilight
Up until dark
The tenacious girl with an undying love
Subdued now with burden of past
Don't quite know
How she lost her flame
Hate blaming game
Afraid to wither
Like a flower its petals
The words jumbled up
Forgot the ink
Voice in shrink

Show me the path again
The love again
Make me forget the pain
Wanna bloom again
Shredded between doubts
Make me rebirth again
It runs in my veins
The pleasure and pain
It's a white thin line, sure!
I will make it this time
Engrave my heart
Oh! Sweet creature
Take me out of my graveyard

25. Nostalgia at its Behest

I love warmth of autumn days
For it helps my sad musing gaze
The seasons of transition
Gives me ambition
Witness new birth ignition
The aura of sleepy hollow
Green leaves turning to amber
Brown, orange and red follows
Melancholy of picturesque fall
Autumnal nostalgia always seems better

Waiting for its downfall
Breaking down like dormant trees
Dry and ruddy as cold cheeks
Nostalgic wistful clouds
Keeps me enshroud
Life is full of quest
Penetrating my thoughts
Soft remembrance at its behest

26. Pale Days

Words fail to come around
On certain pale days
When your memories astound
Simple colourful tassels
Used to twist its edges
To girdle your wrist
A sign of secret unspoken pledge
The fealty of best friends
Our spirits entwined in devotion
Shining on each gold threaded strand
But with the lustres of the day
Came the common shell of darkness
Death took you
Destiny efface us heartless
The lips of death flickered its flame
Took your sudden breath
Left me in the living dark
Bard of blood
Left me like a broken word
But the world moved on
It doesn't stop for anyone
So why grieve?

For life is full of sadness
Dawn will eradicate the darkness
Spring won't dull its brightness
Time won't pause for my numbness
For today seems so long, pale and bitter
But tomorrow shall bring new hopes and glitter
The unlived joys of the present
Will haunt you
Till you resent
You still live in me
In my vision of God's dwell
The subtle murmurs of eternity
My sweet guiding angel

27. Colour of our Sadness

I celebrate the world

That gave me the river

That allowed me to drown in

The same world who gave me the consciousness

Only to submerge in painness

The pain who enlighten me

About the lightness

By making me conscious

About the darkness

It made me realise

That the greatness is full of silence

Only the empty shells make turbulence

Is there any colour of our sadness?

For I found grey

The balance of our madness

28. Thousand Lives

Some feelings are like medicine
But poisonous when expire
Like a blithe desire
But I'm a sinner
I dare to make mistakes
Though if you aren't making any
You will surely regret
Wisdom comes from ache
To those who can relate
Cause I'm aimless
But gravity is the first step
I wanted to revive my wings
But it withered away
Maybe I wasn't supposed to have it
Else it betrayed
Maybe I could've lived
But I was made to die
For I found the earth
Only to fly
Maybe I would've been perfect
But somehow meant to be broken

For I live a thousand lives
That is somehow unspoken
But I never depend on oars
I dive through the sea
Fighting with waves
Floating with breeze
I confront the storms
Eye to eye
With the demons
It's do or die

29. Champagne Eyes

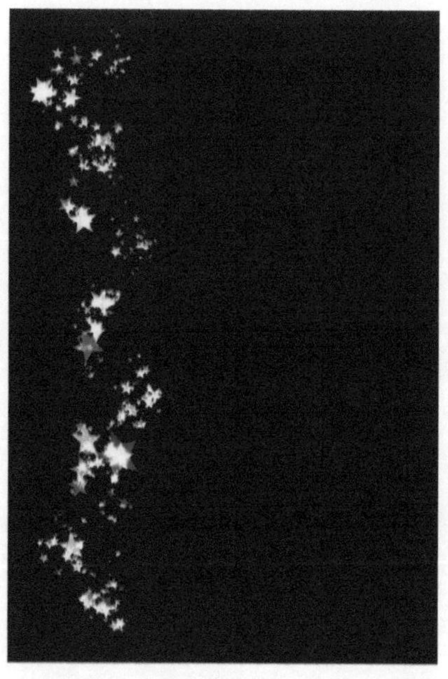

Your champagne eyes are all I want
To make me whole again
To make me feel again
This miserable life will be worthy
If I get to see them again
They whisper to me

To pick up my pieces
That are scattered around like sand
They stare at me
Like I'll never grow old
And be around like a blue ocean
Oh sweet things!
My sweet things!
Let me drown first
And quench my thirst
And I know that I'll cry
But I don't know why
Cause you make me strong
Yet weak at the same time
And make me wanna rhyme
Isn't this a beautiful crime?
Oh sweet things!
My sweet things!
I promise
That even if I feel pain
I'll try to wash it in rain
Come back to me
In the night starry sky
To grow old in your eyes
Cause your champagne eyes
Are all I want
To make me whole again
To make me feel again

Dawn

Becoming isn't always graceful

But it is blissful

You are unaware

Of the strength in your scars

It shows the power

Of the stars

Dig deep

Face the sun

Bloom like a flower

It can be dark

But trust me

Light is still there

30. Ray of Hope

He said alright
I'll show you the path again
Don't you ever lose hope
I'll be by your side in all the pain
He said they'll break you
But I'll make you again
They'll pay for their deeds
You just be you
The truth shall remain
So I said rest assured
Many tears wasted again
With you by my side
I'll fight them
I said
So what I can't see you
In my mind
I see you again and again
The stars taught me
How to find meaning
When it aligns perfectly
Like a bright fountain

31. My Own Kind

My silence is hopeful
Meaningful at times
Golden are the words
Which left unspoken
This breed is different
Difficult to deal
To heal
To feel
To breath
We need this silence
I prefer to speak
Not with just words
But the thoughts
Of my mind
I am my own kind
Kindness is medicine
Spread love and peace
Not hate
That's a disease

32. Million Reasons

Million reasons to quit
Few to survive
Million reasons to lose hope
Few to derive
Words seems to cut deeper
Like a knife
When there's a million reasons
To hate life
Numb… no feelings left
But found a million reasons
To reiterate
The love… to be whole
To find its way in soul
Breathe… it'll come to you
Be the only reason
To beckon the light
The million reasons to believe
In dark Knight

33. A Friendly Star

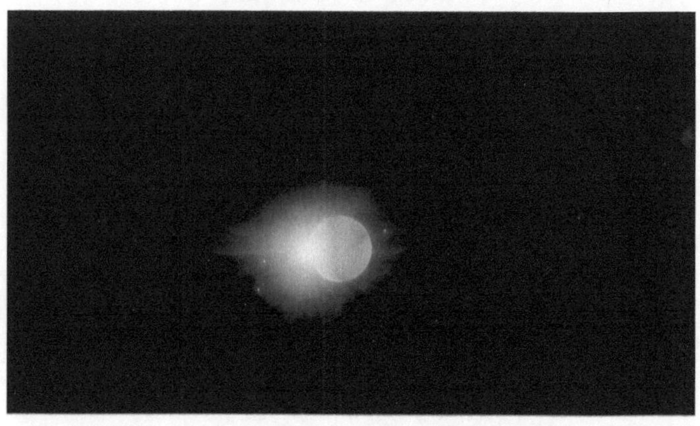

Looking up at a friendly star
She smiled down at me
Burned bright
To shine upon me
She showed me a story
Up at the sky
Wind kissed the clouds goodbye
Born from a chaotic bang
Children of stars
Aren't afraid of ultraviolence

When came into existence
But there was a resistance
In the canvas of vibrant darkness
We came into being
Did aphrodite ever made amend
With athena in the end?
The friendship between
Love and war
As epic as it sounds
I can hear it coming down
For it broke the ground
But amity goes deeper than this
It can be a bliss
If not make you laugh
It can cry for you
If not make you heal
It can suffer with you
If not make you stay
It can escape with you
A true friend is that star
Who can burn for you
While smiling down upon you
Who can show light
When darkness swallow you
Be that friend for someone
If you haven't got one for you

34. Sweet Sorrows of Life

Life is nothing
But an oxymoron
Shattered yet perfect
On its own
Breathtaking mosaic of love and hate
Keep getting defeated
By mere fate
Hate keeps telling me
To be content in its way
You have tried it all
But you keep getting fall
So I lay there for awhile
Only to rise up like a phoenix
In the sky
Like the ocean
I calm myself
For salt water mixed with air
I am too like herself
For I prefer beautiful wild flowers
With full of dew
And the tinge of beauty
Shine upon its petal anew

For diamonds are indeed
Shiny and valuable
But it lacks of warmth
Which is quite undesirable
For I found the light
Brighter than ever
While my soul
Fight through stereotypes forever
Beautiful intricacy of a flower
Depicts the strength of inner power
Faith unfaithfully
Kept me from
A paradox infinitely

35. Wild Flower

I'll be a wildflower

Rare to find

Even harder to crush

Under cruel opinions

No longer waiting for acceptance

Or for validations

Letting my words speak

Simply being who I am

DEBJANI CHATTOPADHYAY

Choosing to see
Through rose tinted shade
Some dreams
Are worth the wait

36. Shrine of Memories

My sorrows has learned to swim
Not letting me drowning in
Poetic musings on a whim
Not allowing my light to dim
My heart maybe colder
But the emotions are bolder

Don't come any closer
Or forget about closure
My heart still beats
For every soul it meets
Like that sweet soul
Who encouraged me to spread wings
Which I clipped long ago
And forced to wring
Or like that stranger
Who taught me
The sweet meaning of rhyme
My life became sublime
My mind is a shrine of these memories
They are more precious to me
Than any accessories

37. Evolution

Evolution is the norm of nature
Change is barbaric
This new me is different
Pieces added brick by brick
I always rise up from dead
But the colour of my soul
Has turned to red
Now I'm drawn to silence
More careful about
The things people don't say
Can handle isolation
When my own heart slay
Isolation is a gift
Others are mere
Test of my patience
But life is all about balance
Forget about clemence
Humanity is barely present
In its glorious absence
Born with empty hands
Will die with empty hands

DEBJANI CHATTOPADHYAY

Yet everyone is fighting
To have a last dance

38. I am Nobody

Don't call me

By my name

I am nobody

Do you know

Who you are?

Or

Pretending to be somebody?

Mere existence

Trying to float

Giving it a name?

Oh please!

Don't gloat!

Just be a graceful soul

Spread kindness, not scars

Keep hatred behind bars

Before becoming

One of the aligning stars

39. Peace will Begin

Write, if you must
But don't let them
Bind you with shackles
Dust, if you must
But stand tall
Like it's free of hassles
Hustle, if you must
In order to become
A fearless queen
So that the darkest hour
Will fear to touch you
Or even dare to dream
Dream big, if you must
Fear will bite the dust
Shadow doesn't last
When your spirit shines
From within
You will move mountains
And the peace will begin

40. Lone Wolf

I am a lone wolf
Drawn to full moon
Full of mystery
A wild flower in cemetery
Floating in foggy air
Come near if you dare
In this game, I'm a pro
Didn't see this coming?
Well now you know!
I'm a silent harmony
Sweet like honey
Might seem uncanny
Blurred between illusion and reality
There's a brutality
In this duality
But these are the realities
We are nothing, yet everything
No use of grieving
I'll bloom like a flower on my grave
So swallow your tears, be brave!
The joys of life is aplenty
I'll keep my last letter empty

41. One Soul

Why should I be a single page
When I can become a story
I'mma be a star
Who wants to be a glory?
I'm burning for a long time
Yours just a spark
Don't think twice
Try to make your mark
Got a single life
Brace yourself and embark
Don't get me wrong
I have seen it all
Don't need anyone
To stand tall

But I know to have someone
Who see your disaster
Who feel you
And help you heal faster
Who kiss your wounds
And cracks of your soul
Who can calm you down
And make you roll
I know that someone is hard to find
But if you stumble upon one
Don't be afraid to
Lose your mind

42. Symphony of Love

Can you hear the music
That I'm dancing to?
It's the symphony of love
Listen carefully
If you want to!
Open your wings
Hide a sword among your pinions
For the path is steep and millions
Don't yield easily
Don't let them see you hustle
Not even an ion
The world is full of opinion
Caught in a wild gamble
Simple souls been burning
But still expected to laugh
Don't let these voices shatter your dreams
Rise above and see them bluff
You are the air and the fire
The water and the earth
The mighty spirit
Who isn't afraid of rebirth

43. Crown of Thorns

And I was drowning one day
Under the weight of my past
Torn pages of the glorified deaths
Horrify me to read till last
And I tried to justify my pain
There is nothing to gain
These depression and anxiety
Will disappear
When I flaunt a smile in chain
Yes! Nobody but me
Keep me chained
And one day I dived in depth
Where most would drown
And I found me
Who wears her pain like a crown
I found me
Who is okay by herself
And don't need anybody else
She can give love to herself
Cause she found
You either fight with the waves
Or die from the thirst

DEBJANI CHATTOPADHYAY

So she chose to fight
Cause that just felt right

44. Dare to be Soft

The world is full of opinions
But don't take me wrong
I'll convey mine in precision
People tend to take
Our silence
For our clemence
Our softheartedness
For our weakness
But make no mistake

We see

What no one can see

Not everyone can hear the music

Which we dances to

We seem insane

So they exclaim

They are in different lane

Blind to our pain

To our gain

Of the euphoric peace

Which we often find in lease

In our easily breakable heart

Which we keep in repair

Cause we care

And we dare

To be soft

Which most are afraid of

45. Searching for Peace

A lot of fight left in me
But I choose to surrender
When all are picking their swords
I choose to look at the stars
Of the constellation
For the peace lies there
Right at the heart
The reminder of healed sufferings
Judging my damnation
I believe in salvation
Keeping in mutation
Karma pays everyone attention
Don't hold on
Turn the page
We must change with age
It's time to uncage
The hidden rage

46. She is Poetry

That she endured
And I found something one day
Stumbled upon poetry, but hey!
I live it day and night
This is not a mere literature to me
It is a priceless emotion
Written in stone
I live through a soliloquy
All the way to the antiloquy
I make them burn me
And shatter all the illusions
For if we want the purity of story
We must go through purgatory
We must get mad and angry
Dive deep and fall in love
Vaguely feel the sorrow
Feel it being painstakingly thorough
Snatch all the words
From the depth of your heart
It will hurt
But it'll be worth it
This is poetry to me
The first step of healing
Before knowing others
Trying to know me
Before letting others
Trying to see me

DEBJANI CHATTOPADHYAY

The warrior in me
Is finally free

Honest things

Doesn't have a colour or a name

It's ever-changing

Like the colour of the wild

Never stays same

The colour of my heart too

Can't be tamed

About The Author

Debjani Chattopadhyay is a poet and a budding novelist. She is a literature enthusiast as she's been a student of the same. Music, poetry and art runs deep in Her bones. She aspires to bring a change through her writings. She believes in spreading kindness and encourages all to do the same.

Debjani has been a part of many anthologies as co-author and turned to an author with the anthology book The Warriors Heart. She has been featured in some prestigious categories such as in Top ten most talented writers of 2021 and in Passion Review magazine September issue 2021.

Debjani lives in Hyderabad with her husband and a beautiful daughter.

She waits for your feedback at debjanimailbox@gmail.com

www.ingramcontent.com/pod-product-compliance
Lightning Source LLC
Chambersburg PA
CBHW020606160726
47991CB00002B/892

मन का सच

(काव्य संग्रह)

मानसिक शांति और स्वास्थ्य का अनूठा प्रतिबिंब

डॉ लव तोमर
(मनोचिकित्सक)

Copyright © Dr Love Kumar Tomar 2022
All Rights Reserved.

ISBN 979-8-88869-644-6

This book has been published with all efforts taken to make the material error-free after the consent of the author. However, the author and the publisher do not assume and hereby disclaim any liability to any party for any loss, damage, or disruption caused by errors or omissions, whether such errors or omissions result from negligence, accident, or any other cause.

While every effort has been made to avoid any mistake or omission, this publication is being sold on the condition and understanding that neither the author nor the publishers or printers would be liable in any manner to any person by reason of any mistake or omission in this publication or for any action taken or omitted to be taken or advice rendered or accepted on the basis of this work. For any defect in printing or binding the publishers will be liable only to replace the defective copy by another copy of this work then available.